natural
water gardens

natural water gardens

Philip Swindells

BARRON'S

First edition for the United States and Canada published in
2002 by Barron's Educational Series, Inc.
First published in 2002 by Interpet Publishing.
© Copyright 2002 Interpet Publishing.

All inquiries should be addressed to:
Barron's Educational Series, Inc.
250 Wireless Boulevard
Hauppauge, New York 11788
http://www.barronseduc.com

International Standard Book Number 0-7641-1850-1
Library of Congress Catalog Card Number 2002101221

Printed in China
9 8 7 6 5 4 3 2 1

THE AUTHOR
Philip Swindells is a water gardening specialist with
a long experience of growing aquatic plants in many parts
of the world. He trained at the University of Cambridge
Botanic Garden and the famous aquatic nursery of Perrys
of Enfield, and ultimately became Curator of Harlow Carr
Botanical Gardens, Harrogate, England. The author of
many publications on water gardening, Philip was also
formerly the editor of the *Water Garden Journal* of the
International Water Lily Society, which in 1994 inducted
him into their Hall of Fame.

The information and recommendations in this book are
given without any guarantees on behalf of the author and
publisher, who disclaim any liability with the use of this
material.

Acknowledgments
The publishers would like to thank the
following people for their help during the
preparation of this book: Anthony Archer-Wills
and Gail Paterson at New Barn Aquatic
Nurseries, West Chiltington; Mike and Wendy
Yendell of Aristaquatics, Billingshurst; Old Barn
Nurseries, Dial Post, Horsham; Stuart Thraves
at Blagdon, Bridgwater; Murrells Nursery,
Pulborough; Graham Quick; Geoff Rogers;
Stonescapes, Cranleigh; and Bulldog Tools.

contents

introduction 6	36 installing a pump and filter
lakes and open water 8	38 making a lined pool
informal garden ponds 10	40 constructing a bog garden
natural garden ponds 12	42 making a wildlife pool
semiformal ponds 14	44 making an island raft for wildlife
bog gardens 16	46 making a clay-lined dewpond
wildlife ponds 18	48 constructing a small stream
water meadows 20	50 edging an informal pond
sunken pools and springs 22	52 pond chemistry
streams and brooks 24	54 what plants where?
cascades and waterfalls 26	56 how to plant in water features
basic principles 28	58 stocking a pond with fish
options and materials 30	60 coping with physical problems
pumps and filters 32	62 ecobalance and seasonal care
installing a rigid pond 34	64 index

introduction

The term natural water gardens could really be applied to three different forms of aquatic feature. All have much in common and there are many crossovers between the three. The true natural water garden is one that is created by nature and is home to native water plants. This is sometimes recreated in gardens and landscapes, but is not the easiest to achieve successfully. In the past, puddled clay was always the material with which a natural excavation was lined, but it is messy to apply and difficult to keep waterproof and in good order. The advent of bentonite powder and bentonite blankets that trap clay between layers of strong textile has done much to popularize natural ponds of traditional construction again.

These water gardens usually accommodate native species of flora that are allowed to develop naturally within loose constraints of regular management. The more vigorous species are occasionally reduced and weaker ones encouraged, but by and large it is a natural environment. This kind of planting is excellent for attracting wildlife, for native species of plants are prime attractions for birds and insects in the vicinity.

The second kind of natural pond is a balanced eco-system of native plants in an artificially constructed pool. This may be made of a pool liner or a prefabricated unit.

The plants can be grown satisfactorily, but the finer elements of a natural pond, like marginal plants scrambling along an earth bottom and producing a tangle of roots into which aquatic crustaceans and other water creatures can burrow and hide, is missing. Such a pond depends for the success of its management upon the use of planting baskets, and while these ensure a fine visual effect, they do to some extent defeat the objective of creating a wildlife sanctuary.

The third kind of natural water garden is a complete compromise: a water feature that has the overall aspect of being natural but is constructed of unnatural materials with an assemblage of plants from the four corners of the globe. The purist naturalist may hold up his or her hands in horror at this prospect, but for the gardener this is probably the best option. It offers a natural look, beautiful blossoms over a long flowering period, and an opportunity for a considerable quantity of wildlife to become successfully established in the garden.

All kinds of natural water gardens offer an enormous amount of pleasure irrespective of the philosophy of the individual gardener. Apart from the individual enjoyment that they give, they also provide important staging posts and sanctuaries for our native fauna, especially in urban districts where life is not always easy.

Above: Moving water – one of the great joys of natural water gardening.
Right: A natural water garden with natural features, but planted with
a handsome array of predominantly garden plants. It is not necessary
to incorporate wholly native species to create a natural effect.

lakes and open water

The large natural pond or lake is one of nature's wonders. Where an existing body of natural water can be incorporated into the garden and enhanced, then the water gardener has the most perfect canvas upon which to paint a picture. Providing that the lake or large pond retains water at a consistent level all year-round, management is relatively simple and the feature remains visually appealing.

In many cases lakes and large ponds have to be created. The advantage of producing your own is that its depth and shape can be predetermined and accommodation made for planting to the desired effect. While such an enterprise requires careful planning, it produces additional opportunities for enhancing the garden landscape by the thoughtful redistribution of soil.

Indeed, where a large body of water is being produced artificially, it is wise to take into account the surrounding garden, even when you are working on a grand scale. The effect of a substantial stretch of water that is introduced into a previously featureless landscape can be remarkably dramatic, not just by its physical presence but also because of the pictures that it creates through reflections.

It is the latter aspect that can be the most visually arresting element, but often the wonderful pictures

produced by nearby trees, buildings, or the scudding of fluffy white clouds across a bright blue sky are overlooked in the planning stage. The effects of the changing seasons must also be taken into account. The

dramatic transformation of a large body of water from a still azure blue mirror in summer to the gloomy gray and choppy surface of windswept winter will have a profound effect on the garden landscape.

Right: A beautifully planted large water garden. Marginal aquatics throng the waterside while clusters of well-maintained water lilies provide a central focus.

Above: A lake that does not depend upon aquatic plants for its beauty. The reflections in the water are the main attraction.

Right: A large natural pond in a garden setting that has been enhanced by the careful management of the surrounding land.

informal garden ponds

The informal pond is great fun for the ardent gardener, for here almost anything goes and a wide variety of plants can be grown without too much consideration for overall visual appearance and symmetry. Most informal ponds reflect nature with regard to their shape and configuration, and planting consists of a tangled informality. They tend to be irregular in shape but they remain evidently part of the garden construct through the explicit use of hard edging, paving surrounds, and so on. In this they differ from

Below: *Tangled informality as plants throng the waterside. Order is brought by the manicured grass edge and the clear open water.*

natural garden ponds (pages 12-13) which strive to mimic the look of a natural body of water, even though they are artificially made.

While such a pond would appear to be very easily maintained, the reality is that considerable care has to be taken over planning and planting in order to produce the casual informal look. Maintenance also has to be both thorough and regular. The end result is well worthwhile, for of all water features the informal garden pond provides the greatest opportunity not only for enjoying plants and fish, but also for creating a whole self-sustaining watery ecosystem.

Just as planting has to be carefully contrived in order to look natural, so too does the pool itself. There is a temptation to produce an intricate mathematical masterpiece with all kinds of fussy niches and contortions. However, such creations are not only a nightmare to construct, but they can be very tiresome to care for. The best informal ponds rely upon sweeping arcs and curves and depend much more upon thoughtful planting for producing the desired effect, although a stone or paved edge assists greatly in defining the pond in its setting.

Left: A pool that gives the enthusiastic gardener the opportunity to grow an extensive range of plants. The marginal aquatics are cleverly contained between stones, which form a hard decorative edge. Soil sculpting in the center permits the unfettered growth of water lilies without incursions from marginal plants.

natural garden ponds

Unlike the informal garden pool, which – although planted in a naturalistic way – is clearly a part of the informal garden landscape, the natural pool brings the informality of the countryside into the garden while allowing you the luxury of eliminating weedy species of native origin in favor of more beautiful water plants of your choice. The natural garden pond emulates the overall visual appearance of the pond found in the corner of the cow pasture with its clumps of reeds and floating water lily pads, but it utilizes garden varieties of aquatics for

Above: A truly natural water garden has extensive moist margins where reeds, rushes, and irises can prosper unhindered. Here a full range of bog and marginal aquatics throng the waterside in great profusion, but none of them advance too far into the pond.

landscape effect. Indeed, to the casual observer the pond and its plants appear to be natural phenomena caught in a garden setting.

The pond itself may be constructed in a traditional fashion, although the puddled clay of a hundred years ago has now been replaced by bentonite clay blankets or bentonite granules. These modern construction materials permit a very natural watertight clay finish to be applied to a pond excavation. Such a method of sealing the pond area is just about as close to nature as it is possible to get and opens up construction opportunities using clay that was

Left: There are few more attractive natural garden features than a waterside tangle of native bog and marginal aquatics mingled with wildflowers. They also attract a rich diversity of insects and birds.

Above: A celebration of aquatic plants and water in a natural setting with adequate provision, in the shape of the bridge and pathway, for everyone to be able to enjoy it to the fullest.

previously a hazardous medium to use because of its propensity for leaking.

Not that the construction has to use natural materials. A pond liner or even a preformed pool can be the basis of a natural water garden if the edges are carefully disguised.

The use of heavy marginal planting that spills over onto surrounding ground is the easiest way to produce the natural look, although allowing grass to grow over the poolside also has its visual merits. Maintenance can be rather tedious, however, for grass requires regular clipping and this can be difficult to do without the cuttings dropping into the water. If such a problem can be overcome, then visually there are enormous benefits in such a method of edging.

semiformal ponds

The semiformal pond is a halfway house between the formal pond with its straight lines, even curves, and open areas of water, and the irregular shape of the informal pond with its great tangle of planting and apparent disrespect for order. Semiformal pools are excellent for helping to provide a transition between house and garden or between more formal areas of the garden and those that are arranged more naturally.

With a semiformal pond an element of formality is discernible, often created by the use of hard landscaping materials, such as paving or stone, especially for the edges.

This gives a clear definition to the pond shape, although rarely is there anything truly formal about the lines and curves. The planting provides the informal element and the marriage of these two aspects has to be very carefully considered before construction begins.

In many ways a semiformal pond can be almost anything that the gardener wants it to be. Providing that it can be clearly seen as an entity with a neat edging defining its

Below: *Natural ponds need not be unruly; they can be well ordered and thoughtfully incorporated into more formal surroundings.*

Above: *This is a pond that successfully occupies the point of transition where the informal and the formal gardens meet.*

Left: *The rugged natural construction of this pool suggests informality, but the structural planting softens the effect to one of semiformality.*

limits, and the marginal plants are grouped in informal array within it, the rest of its design and creation lies in the hands of the gardener. However, as with formal ponds, there is some benefit in keeping an unplanted area of open water, for part of the allure of the semiformal water feature is the way it allows you to enjoy the best of both worlds. The reflections of the sky that are such an attraction of the formal water garden can be appreciated alongside the color and form of a more heavily planted informal pond. It's a beguiling combination.

bog gardens

The bog garden is a valuable adjunct to the water garden, providing opportunities for growing moisture-loving plants that cannot be successfully cultivated in the margins of the pond itself. These are plants that find ordinary herbaceous border conditions too dry and hostile, although a number of them, such as astilbes and hostas, are often established in the open garden.

Apart from offering the enthusiastic gardener a perfect place for indulging a passion for plants that are difficult to grow elsewhere, the bog garden is a visually appealing addition to the natural water garden, although it does not necessarily have to be an integral part of such a feature. Wonderful bog gardens can be created as completely separate garden features and designed in either an informal or formal fashion.

The main requirement for a bog garden is consistent moisture. While really wet conditions can usually be tolerated during the summer months, when winter arrives the soil should be no more than very damp. There should certainly never be water standing on the surface. When a bog garden stands adjacent to a pond, then the water level and moisture content of the bog area can be more easily regulated than if the feature is in isolation and separated

from the surrounding soil by a waterproof membrane.

Successful bog gardens also extend the flowering season at the waterside, for there are several bog plants that start flowering in very early spring and others that continue the season beyond the time when water lilies and marginals are in flower. Some others have colorful autumn foliage.

Above: A well-planted bog garden, in which the upright swordlike foliage of the irises and feathery fronds of the ostrich feather ferns provide summer-long interest.

Left: Candelabra primulas, such as Primula pulverulenta, *are part of the backbone of the late spring- and early summer-flowering bog garden. Primulas are among those bog garden plants that offer the longest flowering period.*

Above: A bog garden should ideally be a natural adjunct to a pond, the water from the pool dampening the soil and helping to sustain the plants.

wildlife ponds

Wildlife ponds take many and varied forms, but in all cases the pond exists as a magnet for wildlife and a resource that the local fauna can enjoy. There are, for example, dewponds that scarcely support any plants in nature but that provide watering holes for animals. When recreated and clay-lined in a garden setting, they can offer some accommodation for plants. Then there are ponds with varying depths for planting that are soil-sculpted to produce open water and a balanced ecosystem, and shallow water bodies that are heavily planted and have little exposed water, but myriad wildlife. The latter are the most interesting to observe, but they are difficult to maintain in good order while retaining their tangled countryside character.

A wildlife pond can develop from virtually any pond, for within days of construction and water being added, the first aquatic insect life will arrive without any further encouragement. When plants are added, more populations will appear quite naturally. However, to create a pond where wildlife is the focus, plant selection should be of species and varieties that attract interesting insects and birds. For the most part these should be native plants, for there is a greater chance of wildlife diversity establishing if natural host and food plants are introduced, although

Below: The marsh marigold, Caltha palustris, *is one of the finest harbingers of spring and a valuable addition to the wildlife pool.*

these are often not the most colorful and interesting from a garden decoration point of view.

Choosing plants that have potential for food and shelter is important and also for creating opportunities for predators to prey upon creatures that are attracted to the plants. Sympathetic pond construction, perhaps by including a cobbled beach or an island, also adds greatly to the likelihood of wildlife visiting the pool and helps an ecologically balanced environment to become quickly established.

Above: *When there is sufficient plant cover, frogs and toads invariably arrive. They capture and eat a wide variety of insects as well as slugs and snails.*

Left: *A wonderful diversity of bog, marginal, and moisture-loving plants. Included is* Pontederia cordata *'Alba,'* Carex, Ranunculus *and* Physostegia virginiana. *All provide cover or sustenance for aquatic insect life.*

water meadows

Water meadows are naturally areas of land in river catchment areas that are periodically inundated with flood water. The water carries with it a rich silt that is deposited over the area, usually sparingly and rather like a fertilizer. Sometimes the river does not swamp the land completely, but the water table is so high that puddles form on the surface of the land and remain there for much of the winter.

Water meadows are noted for their lush grass – not usually of tussocky or vigorously running species, but some of the finer kinds. It is among such a sward that moisture-loving pasture plants such as water aven, *Geum rivale*, globe flower, *Trollius europaeus*, and ragged robin, *Lychnis flos-cucculi*, prosper. A number of bulbs enjoy it too, notably the snakeshead fritillary, *Fritillaria meleagris* and the snowflake, *Leucojum aestivum*.

In a garden setting, a water garden can be established as a lawned extension from the edge of the pond. It is best not to try to convert existing lawn to water meadow, but to set up a proper area, ideally using a fine grass seed mixture and inserting the young plants as plugs into emerging seedling turf in the spring. Some seed companies sell grass seed mixtures with the seeds of native water meadow plants included, but while success for the grass is more or less

assured, this cannot be guaranteed for the colorful flowering plants.

Maintenance of the water meadow is fairly simple. It cannot be treated like a lawn, for regular close mowing will cut out the plants and bulbs. The grass has to be allowed to grow for a

sufficiently long period to permit seeding of the meadow plants and guarantee that the foliage of the bulbs has an opportunity to rebuild its strength. Such areas are treated much as those dedicated to naturalized bulbs and need minimal management.

Right: A water meadow is a long-term project. Careful minimal management allows choice hardy moisture-loving orchids like Dactylorhiza fuchsii *to get established.*

Above: An area of water meadow, which has been enhanced by colorful planting of moisture-loving plants.

Right: Not all water meadows are restricted to native flora. Here a blend of good garden plants like Hosta, Iris *and* Primula *mingle with native wetland species.*

21

sunken pools and springs

Not all natural bodies of water are extensive or planted. Some of the most attractive features are very small and often contain no plants at all. Springs are among the loveliest of such features, especially when they bubble up through a small pool of clear water. Few gardeners have a natural spring in their garden, and even in circumstances where one exists it often manifests itself just as seepage through the soil, rather than the sparkling bubbling spring of fairy tales. With careful excavation and the creation of a small pool surrounding the spring, an attractive feature can sometimes be made, but if a spring effect is what is required, then this is easier to produce artificially.

By excavating and installing a small reservoir, into which a submersible pump can be installed, a bubbling spring can be produced in any small pool or container that is positioned above it. The outlet pipe of the pump can be sealed into the base of the upper container and the water allowed to fill and splash over the sides of the container from which it drains back to the reservoir to be recycled.

Below: *The misty turbulence of this artificial spring supplies the water for a beautifully created cobbled stream that is embraced by clumps of flowering thyme. The fog effect adds a touch of mystery to the source of upwelling water in the central pool.*

Above: A spring in reverse. The water flowing from the wall maintains the level of the cobbled pool. It then gently trickles into the center and to a reservoir from where it is recirculated.

Right: This attractive sunken pool at the base of a stream serves both as a focal point and as a reservoir. The water is pumped from here and recirculated through the stream header pool.

Often, cobbles are used to disguise the surface of the reservoir around the sides of the container.

Similarly, small containers of still water can be used as tiny sunken pools in the garden. There is no point in attempting to produce an ecosystem in them, for such a venture would be doomed to failure. Rather, such small bodies of water are useful staging posts for wildlife in the garden and, where there is insufficient space for a full-scale pond, they offer a useful and charming alternative.

streams and brooks

Streams are important for wildlife, especially the slow meandering kind that trickle over a rocky or stony bottom. All types of wildlife from caddis flies to bottom-feeding fish enjoy a well-cared-for stream. The margins can also play host to abundant insect life if the waterside planting is thoughtfully selected and arranged. Not only are the leafy

Right: *Millstreams can look severe, but attractive planting using* Filipendula, Mimulus, *and* Hemerocallis *softens the edges of this one.*

Below: *A wide, gently flowing natural stream, which has been beautifully complemented by tasteful waterside planting.*

parts of the plants invaluable as a food source and shelter, the roots that trail into the water often provide homes for colonies of aquatic insect life. If a garden does not have a natural stream, then the creation of such a moving water feature might seem a forbidding undertaking. The reality is that a man-made stream is much easier to control and maintain. A natural stream usually flows from a neighboring property and disappears through an adjacent garden so there is little or no control over flow rate or water quality.

An artificial stream can be constructed from preformed stream sections that clip together, or alternatively created as a lined channel. The latter is a particularly good way of producing a very natural-looking stream and ensuring a slow meandering flow. The slope of the stream can be very gentle and the stream bed layered with gravel or pebbles over the liner, thereby producing as close to natural conditions as it is possible to achieve. It also has the benefit that it is easy to clean the stream out thoroughly if necessary.

Most artificial streams use a small header pool and a basal pool to serve as a reservoir into which a submersible pump is installed, the water being pumped to the head of the stream and then allowed to flow gently down from top to bottom.

Right: A stream provides great opportunities for growing a rich diversity of marginal and bog plants. Not only are they a haven for wildlife, but their roots also bind and protect the structural integrity of the banks.

cascades and waterfalls

Natural-looking cascades and waterfalls are attractive visual features in the garden. Rarely do they provide any wildlife benefits, however, except perhaps for bathing birds. Usually rocky constructions, they can be particularly effective on a sloping site, although it is quite possible to alter the lie of the land to make provision for them, especially if a pool is to be an integral part of the feature and there is a surplus of excavated soil available to be piled up to make an elevated mound.

Pool liners, which can serve as a waterproof membrane beneath the entire feature, make it possible for very convincing waterfalls and tumbling streams to be created. It is important that as little of the water that splashes around is allowed to escape or else the surrounding soil will become saturated and constant topping up with water will be necessary. Apart from the need to do so because of natural evaporation, it is best to conserve water as much as possible, for the addition of fresh tap water brings minerals with it and these in turn provide sustenance for green, water-discoloring algae.

The rocks that comprise a natural-looking cascade or waterfall must be carefully selected. Ideally for the best effect they should be of local origin, although any hard rock can be used. Soft limestone and sandstone wear away with the constant passage of water and during winter in cold climates they often shale and fracture during frosts. Granites, millstones, slates, and water-worn limestone are ideal.

Few plants enjoy the rough and tumble of a waterfall or cascade, although several ferns and some marginal aquatics like yellow musk, *Mimulus luteus,* and the blue-flowered water forget-me-not, *Myosotis scorpioides,* are quite content with the constant splash of turbulent water.

Right: *Although this appears to be a natural waterfall, it is artificially contrived. The stones are placed to look as natural as possible, the strata of each running in the same plane. The manner in which stones are laid can have a profound effect upon the appearance of a waterfall, for curves and depression in individual stones will affect the way in which the water moves. Planting the edges heavily with moisture-loving plants and shrubs enables the edges of the feature to be disguised in a natural-looking way.*

Left: *Although a waterfall or cascade permits few aquatic plants to become established directly in the water flow, the humidity and splash that is created is appreciated by those that colonize the edges. Primulas are particularly appreciative of such conditions. With artificial construction it is important to ensure that there are sufficient pockets of soil available for moisture-loving plants.*

basic principles

When establishing a water garden it is important to take into account a number of considerations, the most critical one being siting. Ideally, a garden pool, or other water feature where plants are to figure prominently, should be constructed in a position of full and uninterrupted sunlight. For a viable ecosystem to establish, lush plant growth is essential and all aquatic plants must have plenty of light.

Visually, water is always more appealing when situated at the lowest point in the landscape. This cannot always be arranged, but when it can, take care to see that the site is not waterlogged and that the water table does not rise dramatically during the winter. A water table close to the surface of the soil can cause unwanted ballooning of a pool liner, the pressure of groundwater outside forcing the liner away from the poolside or even displacing a pre-formed pool up out of the ground.

It is also essential to know where utilities to the house or other buildings are laid. It is extremely frustrating to be close to completing an excavation and unexpectedly coming across a water or gas main. Conversely, if water or an electrical supply is to be laid within easy reach of the water garden, provisions for their installation must be made before pond construction begins.

Any use of electricity should strictly follow regulatory advice and all equipment must be specifically manufactured for use with water. Nowadays there is a wide range of pumps, lights, and other electrical equipment available that comply with strict codes of practice. This is a very important consideration for the gardener as well as for his or her children; water features are dangerous places for play and suitable precautions should be employed to prevent accidents. Where young children are likely to play in the garden, it may be necessary to fence off the pool or cover it with sturdy wire netting until they have reached an age at which an accidental fall into the pool will not pose a potentially life-threatening danger.

Above and right: These are not good sites for a pool. A low area, which collects water, can cause problems during the winter, the pressure of groundwater ballooning a pool liner or lifting a preformed pool. Tree roots can cause similar problems, and shade and fallen leaves are undesirable.

CALCULATING POOL CAPACITY

It is relatively easy to calculate the capacity of regularly shaped pools. You measure the surface area of the pool (length x width) and multiply this figure by the average depth to come to a figure for volume. If you are working in cubic meters, multiply this figure by 1000 to give the capacity in liters; if you are working in cubic feet, multiply this figure by 7.48 to give the capacity in gallons.

Irregular pools are harder to assess. The best method is to draw the outline shape of the pool accurately on graph paper. You should then count up the number of squares occupied by the pool's surface to enable you to calculate the surface area. Squares that are only partially occupied should be added together to reach the total. It is not 100 percent accurate, but it does give a good indication. This figure is then multiplied by the average depth to arrive at the cubic volume.

Below: *This pond illustrates the problems of building on a slope. Because levels were not properly checked during excavation, the pool is not level. The liner is exposed on the right while water laps the rim on the left.*

Right: *Underground utility pipes and cables can create difficulties during pool construction, especially when they are encountered during excavation. Check where pipes run while planning the pool.*

> WARNING *Electricity and water make a dangerous combination. Ensure that any electrical device running off mains power is protected by a residual current device (RCD) or circuit breaker that will cut off the supply instantly in the event of a short circuit. All external connections should be weatherproof. All cables should be buried underground in deep trenches and ideally protected by a layer of slabs or tiles positioned above the cable to prevent it from being accidentally severed by anyone unwittingly digging in the area.*

CHECKLIST

- Place the water feature in full sun.
- Keep away from overhanging trees because of falling leaves and disruptive roots.
- Keep away from trees of the cherry family, the winter host of the water lily aphid.
- Check the location of existing underground utilities to avoid damaging them during excavation.
- Prepare the site for installation of required underground utilities, such as electricity.
- Visually, water is best placed at the lowest point in the landscape, but avoid waterlogged areas.
- Ensure that the site does not flood. Install a drain if necessary.
- Ensure the provision of suitable depths of water for both deep-water and marginal aquatics.
- Make any preparations necessary to ensure that safety measures can be made to keep children safe.

options and materials

There are many different methods available for constructing water features. No longer are puddled clay or concrete the main materials for producing a waterproof lining. A wide array of man-made linings from PVC and polyethylene to rubber and bentonite matting have revolutionized pond construction. Preformed ponds of fiberglass, plastic, or composition materials offer another simple method of creating a water garden, although these do not give quite the flexibility of design allowed by pond liners.

Pond liners are used to line an excavation that is the shape of the final pond. In many cases pond liners are vulnerable to damage, especially in stony soil, so an underlay has to be provided. This is usually in the form of a specially manufactured fabric fleece, although

domestic products such as thick wads of dampened newspaper or discarded carpet are often utilized.

Streams are most effectively created with a liner, for they can be more imaginatively designed and the levels better controlled than by the use of preformed sections that clip together. Twists and turns in the streambed are also more easily accommodated with flexible liner.

The same applies with waterfall and cascade units. When preformed they have the advantage of being watertight, quick to use, and producing a consistent spread and flow of water, but the materials from which they are made often have a rather artificial appearance. They are not as easy to make look convincing in a natural setting as a liner dressed with well-placed rocks and softened by planted edges.

MAKING PREPARATIONS

This allowance gives you a margin for trimming the liner to size.

Left: Liner size can be calculated by measuring the pool, embracing the depth and any shelves, at the widest and longest points. These figures give the maximum width and length of the liner required. Allow a margin for an overlap all around.

Below right: A neat way of marking out the shape of an oval excavation. An inverted soft drink bottle is filled with dry sand. The string is pulled taut and a sand line is used to inscribe the oval on the grass.

Above: Irregular shapes can be drawn by sprinkling sand freehand

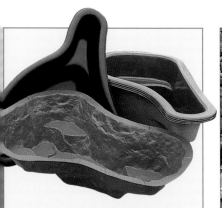

Above: *There are a wide variety of pre-formed pools available in a selection of materials. All are very durable and not difficult to install. Make sure that the marginal shelves are sufficiently large to accommodate planting baskets.*

Above: *Preformed cascade units are easily installed and rarely present any problems with water seepage around the edges. However, they are more difficult to disguise with planting than liner.*

Right: *Preformed cascade units are ideal for small water features. With larger arrangements, the use of a liner and rocks is more desirable. A waterfall using a liner is quite demanding to build if there is to be no water seepage. The arrangement of the levels and the placement of rocks also requires care if the outcome is to look natural.*

pumps and filters

To create both moving water and in order to physically remove suspended pond debris, it is necessary to operate a pump. Pumps are available in an array of shapes and sizes and can be used as the motive force for moving water, creating waterfalls and bubbling springs, as well as operating a variety of filters. Other pumps displace air and can be utilized to oxygenate water.

The most popular kind of pump is the submersible type. This is a sealed unit that is operated by electricity and is completely submerged in the water. Except for the movement of very large volumes of water, this has largely replaced the surface pump that operates from an enclosed chamber adjacent to the pond. Submersible pumps are available with a variety of attachments and apart from straightforward pumping of water from a single outlet are provided with connectors and valves that permit the simultaneous distribution of water through a spring fountain or waterfall.

Above: *This is a multibrush in-pond filter that is operated by a submersible pump. The brushes remove particles suspended in the water while benefical bacteria colonize the filter medium in the bag.*

THE RIGHT PUMP SIZE

When buying a pump it is important that you calculate the flow rate that you need to achieve; this depends on the size of the pool and the number of features that you want the pump to service. For a pump to run more than one feature, you will need to make certain allowances in your calculations to establish the flow rate that your chosen pump must achieve.

Here are some guidelines to help calculate flow requirements:

- A filter requires half the volume of the pond pumped through it every hour.
- A waterfall needs 300 gallons an hour (gal/hr) (1365 liters/hr) for every 6 in (15 cm) of waterfall width required.
- A fountain or ornament requires an extra 30 percent flow.
- An extra 25 percent flow should be added for loss of flow through pipework.

The following two examples show typical setups for which the correct pump must be selected.

Features wanted	Flow calculation	Flow required
9 in (22.5 cm) wide waterfall	(9/6) x 300	= 450 gal/hr
A fountain	450 x 30%	= 135 gal/hr
Allow for pipework	(450 + 135) x 25%	= 146 gal/hr
	Total flow rate needed	= 731 gal/hr

Features wanted	Flow calculation	Flow required
Filter for 594 gal pond	594/2	= 297 gal/hr
An ornament	297 x 30%	= 89 gal/hr
Allow for pipework	(297 + 89) x 25%	= 97 gal/hr
	Total flow rate needed	= 483 gal/hr

When selecting the appropriate pump, you must also make allowance for the maximum head required, for example, the maximum height to which the water has to be pumped above the pond surface. The effective flow rate of a pump will drop off the higher it has to pump water above the pool surface. Ask for advice in your local aquatic or garden center to ensure that the pump you select will be able to provide the required flow at the maximum operational head.

INSIDE A SUBMERSIBLE PUMP

The modern submersible pump can operate a wide range of moving water features. Unlike the traditional pump, which required a separate chamber, the submersible pump is merely placed in the water and connected to the electricity supply.

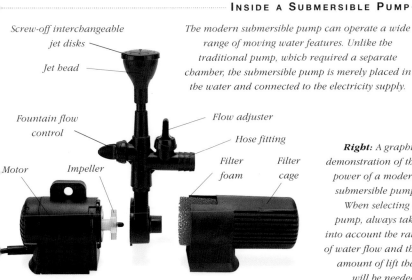

Screw-off interchangeable jet disks

Jet head

Fountain flow control

Flow adjuster

Hose fitting

Filter foam

Filter cage

Motor

Impeller

Right: *A graphic demonstration of the power of a modern submersible pump. When selecting a pump, always take into account the rate of water flow and the amount of lift that will be needed.*

INSIDE A UV FILTER

An ultraviolet filter is a powerful tool for maintaining water clarity, for it destroys all free-floating and suspended unicellular green algae, which are the kinds of algae that give pond water a pea soup-like appearance.

Water inlet

Water out

UV lamp

Submersible pumps require very little maintenance, the periodic disconnecting of the filter over the inlet pipe and washing through of the foam that collects debris being all that is necessary. More elaborate

Left: *A submersible pump can easily operate a fountain. Replacing the disks in the fountainhead alters the spray pattern.*

filters are available. These operate in three different ways. The physical filter extracts and captures debris from the water. This is then regularly removed by cleaning the filter medium. A biological filter is similar but also depends upon biological action of colonies of bacteria to digest waste products in the water. An ultraviolet filter uses UV light to kill off algae and other troublesome organisms.

installing a rigid pond

Rigid ponds are very convenient for water garden construction as all the levels are predetermined and the pond shell is watertight. However, as with all ponds, a little thought is necessary before installation, especially with regard to the lie of the land. It is imperative that when the pond is in its final position it is level from side to side and end to end or else there will be flooding to one side and exposure of the pool wall at the other. Provision should be made for the soil surface to be level before the work of excavation commences.

Once this is achieved, the excavation can be created to suit the shape and size of the pond. Do not try to make it exactly the same size, but allow a little leeway so that when the pool is placed in position small adjustments can be made. This also means that there is room to introduce a cushioning layer of sand and adequate space for backfilling.

When the pool has been positioned correctly and backfilled with sand, check one more time that the levels are correct. The paved edging can then be added. A shallow excavation will be necessary around the edge of the pond to accommodate the thickness of the paving and a shallow mortar bed in which to set it in order to make it secure. This will ensure that the edging and the surrounding grass are level. Raised pond edgings in association with manicured grass create maintenance problems.

1 *Spread sand carefully and accurately around the base of the pool to mark out the shape. Remove the pool shell before digging commences.*

2 *Excavate to the depth of the marginal shelves. Add 2 in (5 cm) all around to allow for the tapered shape.*

INSTALLING A RIGID POOL

Below: The carefully arranged edging stones and imaginative waterside planting hide the fact that this is a rigid preformed pool.

4 *Excavate the entire area. Remove an extra 2 in (5 cm) of soil to allow for a sand base and backfill.*

5 *Remove any sharp stones from the hole. Then cover the shelves with a 2 in (5 cm) layer of building sand.*

(image)

6 *Carefully lower the pool shell into the excavation. Make sure that it is sitting evenly on the sand bed.*

7 *With the pool in position, take a board and spirit level and adjust the pool as necessary to ensure that it is level from side to side and end to end.*

8 *Backfill with sand. This will flow evenly around the shell and support it.*

3 *Place the pond in the hole and mark around the outer edge with sand. This is a guide for the final excavation.*

9 *Once the pool has been installed, excavate around the edge so that a base can be laid for paving.*

10 *Paving is laid onto a layer of mortar on a shallow concrete base. The paving should slightly overhang the edge of the pool to disguise it.*

installing a pump and filter

When installing any filter, other than a straightforward physical or multipurpose filter that sits within the pond, it is sensible to accommodate it separately to the side of the pond. The more complex filters, such as those that are both biofilter and UV filter that will require regular supervision and maintenance, can be best managed in a separate chamber and connected to the pump that operates within the pond.

Take care to ensure that the pump is powerful enough to operate the filter and any feature where water is to be moved. It is always wise to purchase a pump that has 25 percent more capacity than is required. It can always be controlled downward.

Situate the pump within the pond either on the flat bottom or on a suitable plinth. It is important that the pump is level and stable and that it can be easily retrieved from the side of the pond for cleaning and maintenance

on a regular basis. In the setup illustrated here, the outfall side of the pump discharges clean water back into the pond through a decorative fountain, while the input element draws dirty water through the pump to the combined biofilter and UV sterilizer system. Modern pumps connect simply to filters and fountainheads by means of flexible hosing and stainless steel clips.

Apart from the volume of water necessary to operate any decorative feature, it is also important to consider any lift involved. Remember that the pump is likely to be on the bottom, or quite close to the bottom, of the pond and the outfall from an ornament may be 3 ft (1 m) or more above the surface of the water. To assist with this place the pump as close to the outfall as possible. Initially, adjustments will have to be made to the pump until the correct water flow is established and to ensure that there is no wasteful splashing.

COMBINED BIOFILTER AND UV STERILIZER

Water is pumped from the pond into the filter and is forced through a foam block, which extracts floating particles. The bacteria colonizing the foam convert toxic waste products into nutrients, which are available to the plants. The clean water then passes a UV bulb that kills off any algae and parasites.

Unit housing ultraviolet (UV) bulb and electrical connections to run it

Filter for mechanical and biological filtration

Choice of hose sizes, for optimum flow rate

Ultraviolet bulb

Container unit for UV unit and filter foam

Above: *The biofilter can be accommodated in a concrete collar situated beneath the paving at the poolside.*

INSTALLING A SUBMERSIBLE PUMP

1 *Assemble the fountainhead and T-piece. Connect the hose using the largest diameter flexible hose that will fit the pump.*

2 *Tighten up the hose clip so that it does not slip. Do not overtighten as the fountainhead connection may crack.*

3 *Push the T-piece onto the pump outlet. An extension tube can be fitted to lift the fountainhead to the desired height.*

4 *The fountain regulator valve also controls the water flow to the filter. As the fountain flow is increased, the filter flow lessens.*

5 *Position the pump in the pond before connecting to the electricity supply. Connect the hose running from the pump to the inlet on the filter.*

6 *The return pipe taking water from the filter to the pond can be disguised by connecting it to an ornament, here a decorative fish. The pipes can be hidden away beneath the paving slabs.*

Above: *Once the water is running, check that the flow rate through the filter is sufficient for correct functioning. To work out the flow rate, time how long it takes to fill a 2 gallon (10 L) bucket.*

making a lined pool

Making a pool with a liner is probably the most popular construction method. As with a preformed pool, it is essential from the beginning to ensure that the site is level so that when water is added to the pool it does not flood out of one end. Such an error is difficult to rectify once a liner is installed.

Creating the shape of the pool is best achieved by using a length of hose or rope to delineate its shape. This allows you to assess the overall look and proportion of the pool before you start to dig. Spread the hose out on the ground to form the outline of the pool surface. It can be easily adjusted at this stage to produce exactly what is required. Overly decorative corners are generally not desirable as they present difficulties when it comes to putting in the liner and producing a crease-free finish.

A lined pool takes the shape of the final excavation so shelves and levels are created solely from the soil profile. Thus undisturbed ground is ideal for pool excavation. Previously cultivated soil can present difficulties and the collapsing of the pool profile can easily occur. This is also a problem on stony land where the soil structure is unstable. In such circumstances the installation of a pre-formed pond is preferred.

Stones can also be troublesome in a clay or loam soil, especially if they are near the surface, for water pressure within the liner can sometimes lead to puncturing as the stones are forced into the liner. To avoid this, an underlay should be used. It is put into the excavation and dampened so that it clings to the walls. The liner is then spread over this and the pool filled with water. As water is added, the liner should be smoothed out by hand. Creases are best removed as the pool fills as they are impossible to deal with later.

Finally, the edges of the liner are tucked beneath the turf, if you plan a natural planted look, or trapped beneath stones or paving in a semiformal situation.

MAKING A LINED POOL

1 *Mark out the area of the intended excavation with a length of hose. Ensure that the curves are smooth.*

2 *Excavate the pool to the depth of the shelves. These should be deep enough to accommodate a planting basket.*

3 *Excavate the full depth of the pool, digging down from the marginal shelves to create the deepest central pool.*

4 *Level off the floor of the hole using a mattock. Remove any stones or other sharp objects that may puncture the liner.*

5 *Ensure that the marginal shelves as well as the edges of the pool are level from side to side and end to end.*

6 *Place protective underlay into the excavation, molding it to the shape of the hole. This serves as a cushion for the liner.*

7 *Dampen the underlay so that it clings accurately to the shape of the excavation. This makes it easier to install the liner.*

8 *Spread the liner out and try to mold it to the contours of the hole. Make sure to allow sufficient overlap all around.*

9 *Remove as many creases as possible, working from the bottom up. It helps if the liner has been warmed by the sun.*

10 *Add water from a hose. As the water rises and presses against the walls of the pool, smooth out the creases.*

11 *The pool is complete and ready for planting. The liner has been trimmed to shape and tucked under the grass at the edge of the pool. The stones placed around the edge help to hide the top of the pool liner from view along the margin of the shelves.*

Above: *Thoughtful planting not only hides the edge of the liner, but successfully unites the water with the surrounding garden landscape. Marginal aquatics can disguise the edge from within the pool, waterside plants by tumbling over the edge.*

constructing a bog garden

A bog garden can either be an integral part of the water garden or an independent feature in its own right. When placed adjacent to a pond, it is quite simple to use the water in the pond to maintain a suitable level of moisture in the soil by creating a permeable membrane between the two. If the bog garden is to be completely independent, then other arrangements have to be made to ensure constant moisture; otherwise it becomes isolated from the surrounding garden and can in fact turn out to be a drier and more hostile environment for plants.

The construction of a bog garden is similar to that of a lined pool, except that there are no variable depths and the overall excavation need be no more than 18 in (45 cm). Thus it is a shallow basin that is lined either with a pool liner or plain builders' polyethylene. As the lining is completely disguised and there is no direct contact with sunlight that can degrade polyethylene, any cheap waterproof material can be used.

Once the liner is installed, the base should be pricked with a pitchfork to allow excess water to drain away during winter. A bog garden that has standing water on the surface at any time of the year is likely to be a failure. A layer of gravel is added so that the holes will not become sealed by the heavy organic soil that bog garden plants so enjoy.

While watering a free-standing bog garden regularly is one way of ensuring plenty of moisture, the opportunity can alternatively be taken of adding a seep irrigation hose at the stage just before the soil is added during construction. This can be very discreetly introduced and it will not be visible after planting has been completed.

Above: *A bog garden is an attractive addition to a pool or stream. A wide range of moisture-loving plants produce interest from early spring until fall.*

BOG GARDEN CONSTRUCTION

1 *Here the liner for the bog garden is being tacked to a wood frame with felt nails.*

2 *With the liner in place, a pitchfork is used to puncture it to provide some drainage holes.*

3 *A generous layer of gravel is raked over the floor of the bog garden to assist drainage.*

4 *Irrigation hose is put in place so that, when complete, the moisture level can be controlled.*

5 *A richly organic soil is ideal for a bog garden. This is raked out evenly in a thick layer over the gravel.*

6 *The planting of pot-grown plants can take place at any time of the year. In the summer months they must be well watered until established.*

7 *Allow sufficient space between the plants so that they can develop fully and for ease of maintenance.*

PLANTING SUGGESTIONS

Plants Used
Aruncus sylvester 'Kneiffii'/summer/bog
Astilbe taquettii 'Superba'/summer/bog
Hemerocallis 'Black Knight'/summer/bog
Hosta tardiana/summer/bog
Lysimachia nummularia 'Goldii'/summer/bog
Lysimachia punctata 'Alexander'/summer/bog
Monarda didyma 'Petite Delight'/summer/bog
Onoclea sensibilis/spring/summer/bog
Primula florindae/summer/bog
Zantedeschia aethiopica 'Crowborough'/
  summer/bog

Alternative Plants
Iris sibirica/summer/bog
Ligularia clivorum/late summer/bog
Lobelia vedrariensis/late summer/bog
Rodgersia aesculifolia/summer/bog

Below: *An attractively planted bog garden with a rich diversity of colorful moisture-loving plants. Foliage color and form are an added bonus throughout the season.*

making a wildlife pool

Wildlife gardening aims to create places where animals and plants can thrive alongside humans in the domestic environment. A wildlife pool is normally constructed in the same way as a conventional garden pool, especially if the creation of a balanced ecosystem is an objective. However, a layer of soil can be included on top of the liner so that plants can root directly into the soil rather than being confined in planting baskets as is often the case with conventional lined ponds.

The various depths of water necessary for the successful establishment of plants that will produce a balanced ecosystem are essential. Marginal shelves should be provided to accommodate marginal aquatics, and deep water between 18 in (45 cm) and 3 ft (90 cm) in depth is needed for water lilies, other deep-water aquatics and submerged plants, along with sufficient surface area for the free exchange of gases and the establishment of floating plants. Such conditions also provide all that is necessary for fish, snails, and amphibians.

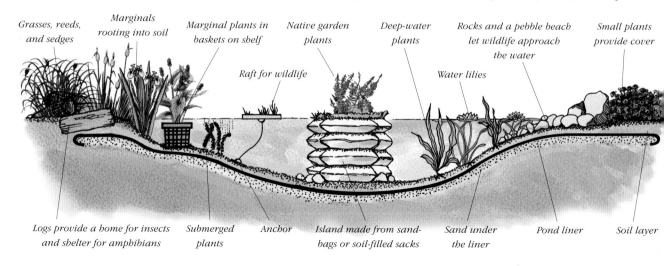

Grasses, reeds, and sedges — *Marginals rooting into soil* — *Marginal plants in baskets on shelf* — *Native garden plants* — *Deep-water plants* — *Rocks and a pebble beach let wildlife approach the water* — *Small plants provide cover*

Raft for wildlife — *Water lilies*

Logs provide a home for insects and shelter for amphibians — *Submerged plants* — *Anchor* — *Island made from sand-bags or soil-filled sacks* — *Sand under the liner* — *Pond liner* — *Soil layer*

MAKING A BEACH

1 *The addition of a beach extension to a lined pool is simple if done at the time of construction. Rake out soil from the excavation from intended water level to the bank.*

2 *Cut the underlay and spread it out from below the water level to the edge of the beach. Dampen it with water to assist with laying and cut off excess.*

The way in which construction is undertaken often differs from that of a decorative garden pool, for unlike the order required in the garden, one of the main attractions of a wildlife pool is the tangled growth of the often ungainly native species. Therefore, planting baskets are often abandoned and the plants permitted to find their place in the pool. If not controlled, a number of the popular weedy species will invade the entire pool. Rather than wait for this to occur, create a pool with a profile that will prevent this from happening. Where areas of open water are desired, sculpt the profile so that at the edge of the desired planted area the water depth exceeds 18 in (45 cm). Very few marginal species will tolerate this and are naturally root pruned where the water becomes deeper.

A wildlife pool is not only about aquatic inhabitants and insect life; there are many birds that can be enjoyed at the poolside if provision is made for them. If a beach is constructed, then they can walk into the water and drink, and they will also greatly enjoy the opportunity of bathing in the margins. A simple wooden ramp also allows small mammals and amphibians easy access to the water.

Right: *A wildlife pond that includes a wide variety of worthy aquatic plants. Such a feature, with a full complement of plants, is likely to retain a naturally sustainable ecosystem. It is doubtless a haven for amphibians, birds, and aquatic insect life.*

3 *Mold the liner to the shape of the excavation, smoothing out as many creases as possible and, if folds are necessary, make them simple and generous.*

4 *Tuck the liner under the turf, and, starting from the upper edge of the beach, use cobbles to create the surface. Use larger sizes at the top of the beach.*

Right: *The beach is complete. A beach gives birds an opportunity to drink and bathe. It also provides a simple exit for frogs and toads and an emergency exit for any adventurous hedgehogs.*

making an island raft for wildlife

Where there is sufficient open water, the provision of an island is a wildlife-friendly measure. Even if quite a modest arrangement, it can provide a peaceful predator-free haven for wildlife, especially birds, and in the rough and tumble of native and associated plantings it offers the gardener an opportunity to isolate more delicate species of plant from the incursion of aggressive neighbors.

Island construction of a traditional kind is a major operation, an exposed area of soil being contained by sandbags or brickwork. Water levels have to be monitored carefully so that it is neither flooded nor the bricks or sandbags exposed, and once planted it is difficult to maintain unless the pool is emptied or the water waded through.

The tethered floating island overcomes all these problems. It offers wildlife the same resources as a conventional island, is not subject to fluctuations in water level, and can be brought to the poolside for refurbishing or inspection whenever necessary.

A wooden pallet or a section of a pallet forms the main part of the structure. Into the gaps in the depth of the pallet empty plastic soft drink bottles are inserted to aid buoyancy and then secured with lumber or wire netting. It is quite a simple matter to cut openings in the surface of the pallet into which planting baskets can be dropped that can accommodate suitable aquatic plants. By confining them to baskets, the plants can be simply lifted for routine maintenance or even changed completely. The provision of a nesting basket and a burlap or sackcloth covering to the slippery wooden surface of the pallet helps to encourage its colonization by waterfowl.

If left to their own devices, floating islands will be blown around the pool by the wind and so it is usual to anchor them to the bottom with a rope attached to a large stone or block.

MAKING A WILDLIFE RAFT

The components needed for making a raft are generally inexpensive and readily available. In this case the materials used are a wooden pallet, some sacking, empty plastic bottles to act as flotation aids, plants and planting baskets, and a wicker basket.

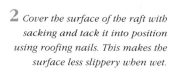

1 *Transcribe the shape of any planting baskets that you want to use in their chosen position onto the surface of the pallet and then cut openings in the wood with an electric saw.*

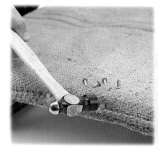

2 *Cover the surface of the raft with sacking and tack it into position using roofing nails. This makes the surface less slippery when wet.*

3 *Trace the position of the holes for the baskets with your fingers and make cross-cuts in the sacking to accommodate them.*

4 *Slip the pots into position. The extra thickness of sacking at the edges will ensure a nice tight fit.*

5 *Arrange empty plastic drinks bottles in the spaces under the pallet. These act as buoyancy aids.*

6 *The bottles can be kept in position by nailing planks of wood along the sides and over the base of the pallet.*

Carex pseudocyperus

Acorus gramineus

Primula denticulata

7 *Plant into the planting baskets using aquatic compost covered with coarse sand. The plants will draw water through the lattice mesh of the baskets.*

8 *Secure a small basket to the top. Once the plants have grown and hidden it, hopefully nesting birds will investigate.*

Remember to tether the raft with an anchor so that you can retrieve it when necessary.

making a clay-lined dewpond

In years gone by, many ponds around the countryside were lined with clay. This involved a complicated and time-consuming process called puddling. Where the soil was at least half clay by volume, pure clay, often of a blue gault kind, was brought in to produce a waterproof lining. Once the excavation had been prepared, it was dusted heavily with soot so that earthworms would be deterred from puncturing it when the clay was laid. The clay was mixed with water, much as a potter fashioning a pot might do, and it was then smeared on the walls of the excavation, starting at the bottom and working to the top. Once complete, the pool was filled with water.

Apart from being a dirty and labor-intensive method of construction, it always had a high maintenance requirement, for unless the clay between the surface of the surrounding ground and the surface of the water in the pond was regularly dampened, then cracks would appear and the pond would start to leak. It was also vulnerable to penetration by the roots of nearby shrubs and trees.

Fortunately, modern clay materials have overcome this, and with the introduction of purified bentonite

Left: Bentonite clay blanket is a remarkable product for lining a pool, for if punctured it is self-sealing. Here a knife has been thrust through the blanket to demonstrate its ability to seal itself around a puncture wound.

LINING A DEWPOND

1 *Mark out the area to be excavated. Use a line and two stakes to inscribe a circle.*

2 *Excavate the hole in the position to the required depth and remove the excess soil.*

3 *Rake over the excavation and remove large stones. Create as even a surface as possible.*

4 *Unroll the blanket, ensuring that there is enough overlap at the pool edge.*

5 *Cut the bentonite blanket to size using a sharp knife. This pond requires two widths.*

6 *Fold back the top layer, and peel the covering from the lower one to expose the clay.*

7 *Flap the top layer down again so that the black covering makes contact with the clay.*

8 *Fold the covering back into place and pat the blanket firmly to make a secure joint.*

10 *The pond can then be filled. A thick layer of soil can be added if you want to add plants.*

Above: *The blanket is made of a layer of clay trapped between two layers of special fabric.*

9 *Once lined, water can be added. This changes the composition of the clay, which can be molded like plasticine. Firming down along the joint creates a seal.*

11 *The edges of the bentonite blanket are then trimmed and neatly tucked beneath the turf.*

clay a similar effect can be achieved much more quickly and conveniently. Bentonite clay is a dry granular material that swells up when in contact with water and naturally seals the soil with which it is mixed, providing that this consists of at least half clay content. For large-scale ponds and lagoons this is ideal, but for the small pond it is not quite so easy to employ.

The alternative is the bentonite blanket that sandwiches a layer of bentonite clay between two layers of textile and that can be purchased in prepacked rolls. It is laid in the excavation in a similar manner to a pond liner. Individual lengths are joined together in a self-sealing way as the bentonite clay will bond to the adjacent sheet as illustrated. When water is added, the joints seal together to make a waterproof lining. Planting can either be in containers, or a thick layer of soil can be added on top of the blanket into which plants can root directly. Pebbles can be used on top of this soil layer as a top dressing to create a more pleasing visual effect.

Above: *Dewponds are naturally occurring ponds that collect water from the surrounding land or are sometimes spring-fed. They are usually devoid of aquatic plants and act as nature's mirrors, reflecting the sky and everything around them.*

constructing a small stream

Streams are best constructed from a pool liner that is disguised completely by rocks, pebbles, stones, and marginal planting. By using a liner it is possible to produce almost any shape or design that is desired. It is also easier to control and adjust the depth and fall of the stream so that the desired water flow is achieved.

The first considerations with a stream are the header outlet and the base pool, for it is difficult to produce a credible independent stream without having a pool at the base in which a submersible pump can be placed and a small header feature to which the water can be pumped. The length of the stream and the ability of the pump to move the water the distance and vertical height required also needs careful thought. It may be that by taking the stream around the garden while keeping its outlet quite close to the header that the pump delivery hose can be

MAKING A STREAM

1 *Mark out the outline of the streambed with stakes or string before digging commences.*

2 *Dig the stream to the full depth taking into account the required slope to the pond.*

3 *Carefully expose the edge of the existing pool, taking care not to puncture the liner.*

4 *Line with underlay, firming it down and ensuring that it molds to the stream's contours.*

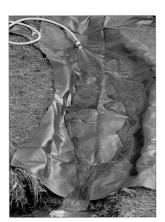

5 *Lay the liner into the trench over the underlay and test that the water flow is satisfactory.*

6 *The pipe that carries the water to the head of the stream is laid in a narrow trench.*

7 *Once the liner has been installed, the stones that form the streambed are laid in place.*

8 *Use large stones piled at the head of the stream to trap and conceal the outlet pipe.*

9 *The pool liner edge is tucked under the turf to create a neat and tidy finish.*

10 *Smaller stones are added to fill in any gaps between the larger slabs on the streambed.*

11 *Lower the pump into the pool close to the stream. It will need to be quite powerful.*

kept much shorter than the overall length of the stream. This is important because the efficiency of the pump drops off the greater the height of the head of water required and the length of hose the water is pumped through.

The liner should ideally be all in one piece – rather than separate overlapping lengths – and it should be laid into a shallow excavation. It must also be spread well over the sides and tucked into the turf or concealed with edging material. If several pieces of liner do have to be used, ensure a generous overlap with the upper pieces overlapping the lower ones in the same manner as roof tiles. Once lined, the streambed should be heavily dressed with slabs of stone and pebbles. Similarly, large rocks and stones can be used to hide the sides of the stream, while occasionally provision can be made for a marginal plant to be established to assist in the disguise of the stream edges.

The flow of the stream can be greatly enhanced by the placement of attractive rocks in its course. These can be used to narrow the stream and squeeze the flow so that it tumbles faster, or placed in a position where the water dances over them and creates splashes and highlights.

Right: *An artificial stream is so much easier to manage than a natural one, yet with clever planting and the suitable placement of stones it can appear quite natural within its garden setting.*

edging an informal pond

The edge of a pool is important, for it defines the water body visually and also provides a secure place to stand and enjoy the fruits of one's labor. Often, it is the transition from pool to garden that ruins the overall effect of a water feature. Carefully constructing the edge, the point where pool meets land, will be the first step in the right direction.

Paving is one of the most popular forms of edging and, if laid properly, it is secure, good looking, and maintenance-free. Whether the pool is of liner or preformed construction, the surrounding ground should be reduced by the combined depth of the proposed paving stone and mortar bed. This assumes that the edge of the pool is at the level of the bottom of the mortar base. If it is at ground level, then soil will need to be built up behind the paving.

There is a great diversity of paving materials available for the home gardener. Not just square or rectangular slabs, but ones cut at an angle so that a curve can be easily achieved. When an informal pool is going to have some fairly eccentric curves and arcs, it is sensible to have a look at the variety of shapes that paving slab manufacturers can supply before deciding upon the shape of the pool.

Of course, if the pool already exists and the paving is a later addition, or you have a new pool but must use landscaping materials that match other garden features, cutting to shape may be necessary, a cold chisel being the best tool for the job. Paving is laid on a generous bed of mortar, each slab protruding slightly over the edge of the pool to assist in its disguise. Each slab should be level and the gap between be pointed with mortar.

Not all edging has to use hard materials; an informal pool looks very effective with grass running up to the water. While this can be quite natural, with the pool liner tucked under the existing turf, another option is to establish turf on a layer of rock wool (a type of building insulation material). This can be brought right to the edge of the water and consolidated over the liner.

EDGING A POND

1 It is important to lay paving stones on a firm base. Make a concrete mix with coarse builders' sand and cement, six parts to one by volume. Mix with water until a sticky agglomeration forms.

2 Excavate the soil around the pool edge so that the concrete base can be spread. The slabs are usually laid on a mortar bed comprising three parts by volume bricklayers' sand and one part cement.

3 At one point in the paving, insert a short length of plastic pipe between the paving slabs. This will permit access for an electrical cable if a pump or lights are to be installed later.

4 *Mortar is spread out with a trowel, taking care not to let it drop in the water. It should be about 1 in (2.5 cm) deep.*

5 *Ensure that the paving slabs are level and also provide a small overhang at the edge.*

6 *If the paving slabs are a little high they can be gently tamped down by tapping them with the handle of a hammer.*

7 *Occasionally it may be necessary to cut a paving slab. This is best done on a soft base using a hammer and cold chisel.*

8 *The paved edging is nearing completion. The overhang provided by the paving slabs hides the liner.*

9 *Cut slabs should be used to ensure that the paved edge has a neat outline. Carefully bed them into the mortar.*

10 *Point the joints between the paving slabs with mortar. This not only provides a finish, but also secures them.*

11 *Dragging an old metal bucket handle or piece of pipe along the joints can neatly finish the surface of the mortar.*

Above: *The paved edge makes a secure, neat finish and also provides a visual frame for the in-pool planting.*

pond chemistry

Understanding the chemistry of the pond is important if a good quality of water is to be maintained. If there is no overstocking of fish and plants are installed in numbers and varieties that ensure a natural balance, then there are few problems. However, it is good to be aware of what can go wrong and why.

Problems mostly occur if the plant population goes into decline and fish population levels rise. This can have an adverse effect upon the nitrogen cycle. It is the lack of control of nitrogenous wastes deriving from the fish that can lead to problems, especially a rise in ammonia levels.

In nature, nitrifying bacteria break down toxic wastes into less harmful products. This takes place as part of what is known as the nitrogen cycle. Organic material usually contains proteins in variable amounts. When protein is broken down either by bacterial decomposition or as a waste product of protein metabolism, ammonia is formed. Bacterial action converts ammonia, which is extremely toxic to fish, into less toxic nitrites. These in turn are converted into nitrates that are relatively harmless substances that are taken up as "food" by plants and used in the construction of plant proteins. The process of converting ammonia into nitrate is called nitrification.

When there are considerable numbers of fish, this process, which naturally occurs in the pond, will benefit from the action of a biological filter. Such a filter provides a home for beneficial bacteria to prosper. Even when the water chemistry of a pond appears to be healthy, it is wise to check periodically for nitrites. Most garden centers offer simple test kits that can be easily used by the gardener.

The digestive processes of fish break down plant proteins and create ammonia as one of the waste by-products.

Plants absorb nitrates, which are used to produce proteins.

Aerobic bacteria oxidize and convert nitrite into nitrate.

Ammonia is tox and present bot in fish excretion and decaying food and plant material.

Aerobic bacteri oxidize harmful ammonia, converting it int less toxic nitrite.

The Nitrogen Cycle *This is how nitrogen circulates in a pond. The bacteria that convert one nitrogen-containing compound into another occur naturally. It is essential to encourage them to thrive in filters to prevent ammonia and nitrite from building up.*

They involve mixing a small sample of pond water with a chemical that then turns color and is compared with a test chart. There is a similar test that can determine the relative acidity or pH of the water. Although this is rarely as critical for nitrite, it is useful to keep an eye on the acidity of the water.

While a natural balance of plants and sensible stocking leve with fish is the most satisfactory method of maintaining stability, the introduction of physical, biological, and UV filter can be recommended, depending upon circumstances. Using an air pump to improve the oxygen content of the water is also invaluable, especially where there is a heavy population of fish. These resemble aquarium pumps and they can improve water quality considerably, especially in the murky, often lifeless, bottom of the deeper pool.

TESTING POND WATER

1 *The testing of pond water should be carried out routinely. It is essential to obtain a typical fresh sample in a small test tube.*

2 *For a pH test for water acidity a tablet is dissolved in the water sample. This colors the water, which is then matched against a chart.*

3 *The results of most pond water tests are analyzed against a graduated color chart of comparative readings. The sample on the left shows a broad-range pH reading, while that on the right gives the result of a simple test for nitrite levels in the pond water.*

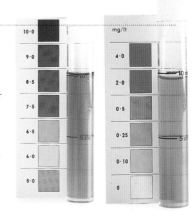

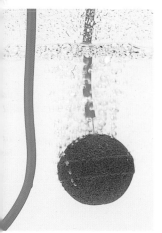

Above: *An air pump dissipates oxygen through the water. This is helpful to fish and improves water quality.*

Above: *A UV filter is extremely valuable for the control of algae suspended in the water.*

Above: *A very healthy, well-planted, and carefully maintained pond demonstrating how good water quality can benefit its inhabitants. The water has a clear reflective appearance that indicates that it is well oxygenated and in excellent condition.*

what plants where?

There are many plants that can be used in a natural water garden, but if attracting wildlife is a main objective, it is usual to concentrate on native species, even if they are a little less showy. Plants from other countries and continents may prove to be a mecca for insects and birds, but the planting of native kinds always enhances the prospects for successful wildlife interaction.

Where wildlife is not a prime concern, but a rugged natural look is the objective, then it really does not matter what species or varieties are used. Their visual attributes are paramount, but they should still be introduced in a

MARGINAL PLANTS

Butomus umbellatus **(flowering rush)**/pink/late summer Height 60-90 cm (2-3 ft). Spread 30-45 cm (1-1½ ft). Depth up to15 cm (6 in).

Carex pendula **(pendulous sedge)**/brownish (also almost evergreen foliage)/summer Height 45-60 cm (1½-2 ft). Spread 45-60 cm (1½-2 ft). Depth up to 10 cm (4 in).

Calla palustris **(bog arum)**/white/summer Height 15-30 cm (6 in-1 ft). Spread 10-15 cm (4-6 in). Depth up to 10 cm (4 in).

Caltha palustris **(marsh marigold)**/yellow/spring Height 30-60 cm (1-2 ft). Spread 10-15 cm (4-6 in). Depth up to 30 cm (1 ft).

Iris laevigata/blue/summer Height 60-90 cm (2-3 ft). Spread 30-45 cm (1-1½ ft). Depth up to 15 cm (6 in).

Iris pseudacorus/yellow/summer Height 90 cm-1.2 m (3-4 ft). Spread 45-60 cm (1½-2 ft). Depth up to 25 cm (10 in).

Lysimachia nummularia/yellow/summer Height 2.5 cm (1 in). Spread 30-45 cm (1-1½ ft). Depth up to 10 cm (4 in).

Myosotis scorpiodies **(water forget-me-not)**/blue/summer Height 20-25 cm (8-10 in). Spread 10-15 cm (4-6 in). Depth up to 10 cm (4 in).

Pontederia cordata **(pickerel)**/blue/late summer Height 60-90 cm (2-3 ft). Spread 30-45 cm (1-1½ ft). Depth up to 15 cm (6 in).

Typha minima **(dwarf Japanese bulrush)**/brown fruiting heads/fall Height 45 cm (18 in). Spread 15-20 cm (6-8 in). Depth up to 10 cm (4 in).

Veronica beccabunga **(brooklime)**/dark blue/summer Height 15-20 cm (6-8 in). Spread 10 cm (4 in). Depth up to 10 cm (4 in).

SUBMERGED PLANTS

Height is not applicable to these plants and spread is unpredictable. They will tolerate water between 30-90 cm (1-3 ft) in depth.

Elodea canadensis **(Canadian pondweed)**/evergreen foliage/all year-round.

Hottonia palustris **(water violet)**/white lilac flowers/summer.

Lagarosiphon major **(goldfish weed)**/evergreen foliage/all year-round.

Myriophyllum aquaticum **(parrot's feather)**/finely cut blue-green foliage/spring/summer.

Ranunculus aquatilis **(water crowfoot)**/white-gold flowers/summer.

BOG GARDEN PLANTS

Astilbe arendsii **hybrids**/red, pink, white/summer Height 45-90 cm (1½-2 ft). Spread 25-45 cm (10in-1½ ft).

Cardamine pratensis **(cuckoo flower)**/rosy-lilac/spring Height 30-45 cm (1-1½ ft). Spread 15-25 cm (6-10 in).

Filipendula ulmaria **(meadowsweet)**/creamy-white/summer Height 60 cm-1.2 m (2-4 ft). Spread 30-60 cm (1-2 ft).

Hosta fortunei **(plantain lily)**/lilac/violet, grayish foliage/summer Height 60-90 cm (2-3 ft). Spread 30-45 cm (1-1½ ft).

Iris ensata/purple/summer Height 60-75 cm (2-2½ ft). Spread 30-45 cm (1-1½ ft).

Matteuccia struthiopteris **(ostrich feather fern)**/green foliage/summer Height 90 cm (3 ft). Spread 45 cm (1½ ft).

Primula candelabra **hybrids**/many colors/summer Height 60-75 cm (2-2½ ft). Spread 30-40 cm (1-1⅓ ft).

Rheum palmatum **(ornamental rhubarb)**/white/summer Height 1.5-1.8 m (5-6 ft). Spread 75-90 cm (2½-3 ft).

Zantedeschia aethiopica **(arum lily)**/white/summer Height 60-75 cm (2-2½ ft). Spread 30-45 cm (1-1½ ft).

way that enables a natural ecobalance to be maintained, particularly within the water body.

Marginal aquatics provide much of the poolside decoration, but submerged aquatics are vital in mopping up excessive nutrients from the water where they encourage the development of water-discoloring algae, while floating plants and deep-water aquatics reduce light falling beneath the water and make it difficult for algae to become established.

FLOATING PLANTS

These have negligible heights and spread is unpredictable. They will tolerate any depth of water over 15 cm (6 in).

Hydrocharis morsus-ranae (frogbit)/white/summer.
Stratiotes aloides (water soldier)/pinkish/summer.
Trapa natans (water chestnut)/white/summer.
Utricularia vulgaris (greater bladderwort)/yellow/summer.

DEEP-WATER AQUATICS

Aponogeton distachyos (water hawthorn)/white and black/late spring/fall Spread 30-90 cm (1-3 ft). Depth 30-90 cm (1-3 ft).
Nuphar advena (American spatterdock)/yellow/summer Spread 45 cm-1.5 m (1½-5 ft). Depth 45 cm-1.5 m (1½-5 ft).
Nuphar lutea (yellow pond lily)/yellow/summer Spread 30 cm-2.4 m (1-8 ft). Depth 30 cm-2.4 m (1.8 ft).
Nymphoides peltata (water fringe)/yellow/summer Spread 30-75 cm (1-2½ ft). Depth 30-75 cm (1-2½ ft).
Orontium aquaticum (golden club)/gold-white/summer Spread 45 cm (1½ ft). Depth 45 cm (1½ ft).

WATER LILIES (ALL FLOWER DURING SUMMER)

Nymphaea 'Arc-en-ciel'/pink with variegated foliage Spread 45-90 cm (1½-3 ft). Depth 45-90 cm (1½-3 ft).
Nymphaea 'Charles de Meurville'/plum-red Spread 1.2-1.8 m (4-6 ft). Depth 1.2-1.8 m (4-6 ft).
Nymphaea 'Escarboucle'/crimson Spread 30-60 cm (1-2 ft). Depth 30-60 cm (1-2 ft).
Nymphaea 'Hermine'/white Spread 30-60 cm (1-2 ft). Depth 30-60 cm (1-2 ft).
Nymphaea 'Gladstoneana'/white Spread 1.2-2.4 m (4-8 ft). Depth 1.2-2.4 m (4-8 ft).
Nymphaea 'Marliacea Albida'/white Spread 45-90 cm (1½-3 ft). Depth 45-90 cm (1½-3 ft).
Nymphaea 'Marliacea Carnea'/pink Spread 1.2-1.8 m (4-6 ft). Depth 1.2-1.8 m (4-6 ft).
Nymphaea 'Marliacea Chromatella'/yellow Spread 45-75 cm (1½-2½ ft). Depth 45-75 cm (1½-2½ ft).
Nymphaea 'Rose Arey'/pink Spread 45-75 cm (1½-2½ ft). Depth 45-75 cm (1½-2½ ft).
Nymphaea tuberosa 'Richardsonii'/white Spread 1.2-1.5 m (4-5 ft). Depth 1.2-1.8 m (4-6 ft).

how to plant in water features

There are two main methods of establishing aquatic plants, other than planting directly into an earth pool floor. Both enable reasonable control to be exercised over the growth and development of the plants and permit the use of appropriate compost that ensures lush growth without encouraging the water to turn green with water-discoloring algae.

It is essential that aquatic plants are grown in natural heavy soil or compost. Specially prepared aquatic compost is ideal as a suitable slow release fertilizer is included that is readily available to the plants as they require it, but not so soluble that it adds sufficient quantities of nutrients to the water to produce an algal bloom.

Container planting is the most popular method and easiest to manage. Aquatic planting baskets are of a latticework construction to prevent the compost from turning sour when totally submerged. Modern latticework materials are of a micromesh structure and do not permit the compost to pollute the water. Older baskets have quite large mesh and benefit from lining with burlap before the soil is added.

The compost is dampened and the aquatics planted. Further compost is added and the basket is watered to drive out the air. A layer of pea gravel is scattered over the top. This prevents soil from escaping into the water and discourages fish from poking around in the container and stirring up the compost that muddies the water.

Plants can also be established with a simple wrapping method using burlap and compost. A square of burlap is laid flat and a mound of compost placed in the center. The plant is positioned and then tied up as if in a package. This is then placed into the water. Eventually the roots completely surround the burlap package.

PLANTING AN AQUATIC

1 *Tidy up the plant, removing any dead leaves. Fresh foliage will grow after planting, which should take place in spring or summer.*

2 *Remove excess roots. Do not be nervous about reducing them by about half, as many of them would die back anyway.*

3 *Use a proper aquatic planting basket and plant firmly into either a proprietary aquatic compost or clean, heavy, garden soil.*

4 *Top up the basket with a layer of well-washed pea gravel. This helps to prevent soil from escaping into the water and also fish from stirring up the compost as they look for food.*

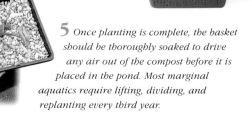

5 *Once planting is complete, the basket should be thoroughly soaked to drive any air out of the compost before it is placed in the pond. Most marginal aquatics require lifting, dividing, and replanting every third year.*

NATURAL PLANTING

1 Where an earth-bottomed pool is to be planted, or where the marginal shelf is very narrow, plants can be wrapped in burlap. Take a square of burlap and place the plant in the center with some compost. Trim off dead growth.

2 Wrap the root and the compost in the burlap square and tie it neatly around the crown of the plant without causing any damage to the leaves.

3 Place the package into the water. The roots will penetrate the compost and the burlap. In a natural earth pond they will then advance into the surrounding soil.

Above: *An established pond with water lilies and iris thriving in their habitat.*

stocking a pond with fish

No natural pond would be complete without its complement of fish. Apart from bringing life to the water, they help to control undesirable aquatic insect life such as mosquito and gnat larvae. They also feed on daphnia, caddis flies, and other forms of aquatic life that in the more natural pond are regarded as a bonus. In the garden pond caddis flies are a pest, for they strip the foliage of aquatic plants. Conversely, in the wildlife pond they are a fascination, for each constructs itself a shelter in which to live out of plant debris and stones. Different species each build a unique kind of shelter.

While fish are useful, it depends upon personal aspirations as to how many are introduced and of which species. Goldfish are extremely useful and resilient. So too their fancy variety, the shubunkin, and the comet-tailed forms of each. Golden ide (orfe) and both golden and silver rudd are attractive fish that tend to shoal and live toward the surface of the pond. Tench are fish that live on the floor of the pond and are referred to as scavenging

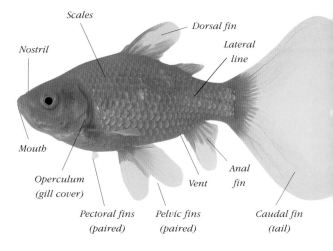

Scales

Dorsal fin

Lateral line

Nostril

Mouth

Operculum (gill cover)

Pectoral fins (paired)

Pelvic fins (paired)

Vent

Anal fin

Caudal fin (tail)

fish. They rarely show themselves, and although interesting characters, are of dubious decorative merit.

Before fish are introduced to a pool it is wise to disinfect them. Use a product based upon methylene blue and

INTRODUCING FISH TO A POOL

 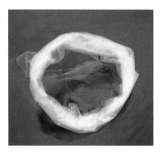  

1 *Prepare fish before introducing them to the pool by equalizing the water temperature in their bag with that in the pool. Roll down the top of the bag to make a collar.*

2 *Float the bag containing some of the original water in which the fish were purchased on the surface of the pool. The temperatures will begin to equalize after several minutes.*

3 *Pour some pond water into the bag to assist with the temperature equalization process and to adjust the relative pH levels. Leave the bag for another 20 minutes or so.*

4 *Once the temperature has equalized within the bag, the fish can be gently poured into the pool. For the first few days after introduction they may not be very visible.*

Above: *When freshly purchased fish are introduced to a pond, it is prudent to disinfect them with an antifungal and antibacterial solution. This ensures that they do not bring infection to your pond.*

STOCKING LEVELS

The guideline for the maximum stocking level of a pond is 0.8 in (2 cm) of fish per 11 gallons (50 L) of water. So a pond holding 440 gallons (2000 L) of water will support 31.5 in (80 cm) of fish – four fish each 8 in (20 cm) long or eight fish each 4 in (10 cm) long etc. However many fish the pond will theoretically hold, always understock to allow the fish to grow to the natural stocking level of the pond. Overcrowding results in poor growth and outbreaks of disease.

If you are stocking a new pond, allow some days to elapse after filling it with water before you introduce fish. This allows the water chemistry to settle, the filter time to get working, and plants the opportunity to establish themselves.

Above: *Nishiki koi are very popular fish and are much prized by pondkeepers. Unlike goldfish, koi are quite boisterous and when present in quantity can ruin a well-planted pond.*

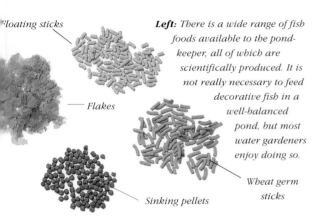

Floating sticks

Flakes

Sinking pellets

Left: *There is a wide range of fish foods available to the pondkeeper, all of which are scientifically produced. It is not really necessary to feed decorative fish in a well-balanced pond, but most water gardeners enjoy doing so.*

Wheat germ sticks

immerse them in it before returning them to a small bag of water and floating this on the surface of the pond. After a short time, when the temperature of the water inside the bag has equalized with that in the pond, release them into the water as illustrated on the opposite page.

Fish do not have to be fed in a pool that is well stocked with plants and where there is a balanced population. However, few people can resist the temptation of feeding and this can become a regular summer ritual. There are many good foods around varying from flake and floating pellets to the more traditional biscuit meal and sinking pellets.

coping with physical problems

Water features have problems from time to time, irrespective of how carefully they are constructed and maintained. The worst possible problem is a leak. Not that leaks are difficult to repair for there are repair kits for most water gardening systems. It is finding the leak that causes the greatest difficulty.

The water level usually falls to a point level with the leak. By removing a quantity of water to take the level within the pool a few inches lower, the source of the problem is often exposed.

1 *Periodically a beach requires cleaning. Dirt gets between the stones and areas that are constantly wet gather algae.*

2 *Remove all the stones and wash them thoroughly by hand. Hose down the beach area and then replace the cobbles.*

REPAIRING TORN LINER

Backing tape

Self-adhesive repair tape

Original liner

The first sign of a problem is usually when the water drops to the same level after the pool has been filled several times. If a leak is suspected, lower the water a few inches and the tear will usually be exposed. Tears usually have to be repaired in situ. Clean the liner thoroughly and allow it to dry. Purchase a suitable repair kit for your liner. There are specific repair kits, rather like those used for mending bicycle tire punctures, for PVC or rubber. Take a suitable size patch to cover the area of the tear completely, press it down firmly, and buff it down to secure the seal. Allow it to dry thoroughly before refilling the pool with water.

Fiberglass preformed pools are not so widely used now, but in the past they were among the most popular forms of pool construction. Many have been in the ground for a number of years. Following routine maintenance, when the gardener has often stood in the pool, a crack will appear. It is rarely severe damage, but sufficient to cause irritating seepage. If properly cleaned and dried, this is easily repaired with a do-it-yourself auto body repair kit.

There are specific pool repair outfits for rigid plastic and preformed pools, while kits that resemble those for repairing punctures are commonly available for rubber, LDPE, and PVC pool liners. Take care to obtain the correct kit for the liner and then clean the damaged area thoroughly. Dry if off and apply the patch. Concrete ponds also suffer from leaks. While many fewer are constructed now than in the past, there are large numbers still providing gardeners with pleasure. When repairing a concrete leak, it is important to chisel out around the damaged area and to replace with quick-drying cement. Once the cement has dried properly it can be painted over with a pond sealant.

Above: A well-planted pool where the marginal planting has secured the edges from erosion. The water quality is good and everything looks healthy, although the water lilies are going to require lifting and dividing next spring. The rising foliage of water lilies above the surface of the water is a sign that they are becoming too crowded.

With natural water features erosion can be a problem, especially when the pond is of natural construction. Larger pools can suffer from wave erosion and even small domestic streams show signs of sheet erosion. This is when water is forced to pass around corners too quickly and bounces from one side of the stream to the other. Planting usually overcomes these problems, densely rooting marginal aquatics like *Mentha aquatica* and *Veronica beccabunga* being ideal to bind the soil together.

Pumps and filters rarely cause problems. Pumps should be regularly inspected and any debris removed. When necessary, filters must be cleaned and filter materials replaced. If there is a fault with the pump and it does not function properly after usual routine maintenance has taken place, then discard it, for modern submersible pumps are far better and more safely replaced than having repairs done to them.

Right: A pump must be cleaned regularly. Filamentous algae clings to most objects in a pool if given the opportunity. This greatly impairs its efficiency.

ecobalance and seasonal care

The ecobalance of a water feature once established has to be maintained. It is important to ensure that the balance of submerged subjects and both floating plants and the foliage of deep-water aquatics are controlled satisfactorily. Marginal plants, although of no great significance in maintaining a balanced ecosystem, can disrupt it considerably if allowed to spread indiscriminately. So the regular lifting, dividing, and trimming of plants is essential both during the spring and into the summer.

Algal growth presents a problem for every pool owner at some time, even if it is only during the first few weeks of early spring when the water has warmed up and the submerged plants are not actively growing and competing with them for mineral salts. Aquatic algae appear in many forms, but there are two main kinds; the free-floating and filamentous. The free-floating kinds are those that occur in great masses and give the water an appearance of pea soup. The filamentous kinds appear as thick masses of silkweed or blanketweed. There are other species such as mermaid's hair that cling to the sides of the pond and to containers, but they enhance rather than detract from the natural water garden.

The best solution for algal problems is to create a natural balance with plants providing competition with algae for nutrients, and surface foliage shading out suspended algae. Chemical controls work, but are only temporary solutions. However, they can be very useful early in the life of the pool while the main plants that are to provide the balance become established. When algicides are used to kill filamentous algae, then the dead algae must be removed so that it does not deoxygenate the water.

Leaves are also a great problem for pond owners. Natural ponds visually can tolerate a few more than more formal arrangements, but not when it comes to an accumulation

REGULAR MAINTENANCE

Above: *The occurrence of slime and algae cannot be avoided, even in the best-balanced pools. Throughout the summer it is necessary regularly to remove filamentous algae with a net by hand or by twisting it around a cane. Algicides can be used but dead algae still has to be removed or it decomposes and deoxygenates the water.*

Below: *Fallen leaves are a nuisance in a pond, especially at autumn leaf fall. They rapidly sink to the bottom where they slowly decompose and pollute the water. Netting over the pond, or erecting a temporary fence around it to prevent leaves from blowing in is the best preventative. During the summer fallen leaves should be netted out by hand.*

Above: *As winter approaches it is important to clean up the waterside. Any dead or decaying foliage on marginal or moisture-loving plants should be removed. Faded foliage should be cut back to the ground, but marginals, especially hollow stemmed species, must not be cut below the water level or else they may rot.*

These include those of the horse chestnut family (*Aesculus*), which are particularly noxious, as well as willows (*Salix*), which have properties similar to aspirin and can harm fish when they decompose in the pool.

The temporary use of netting to protect the pool from fallen leaves is the best way of keeping them out. Covering the pool completely is often recommended, but this is both unsightly and can damage the marginal plants. It is more satisfactory to use small mesh netting about 18 in

Above: *During winter spray dormant plum and cherry trees with a winter wash. These are the overwintering host of the troublesome water lily aphid. Killing the eggs at this stage breaks the life cycle.*

(45 cm) high and to fasten this to stakes around the pool. This prevents the majority of leaves from entering the water as the greater number blow into the pool from the surrounding garden, rather than fall directly from the trees into the water. Small quantities can be scooped out.

During the winter it is important to winter-wash fruit trees of the plum and cherry (*Prunus*) family, for these are the overwintering host of one of the most troublesome aquatic pests, the water lily aphid. During the fall adult female aphids migrate to the trees and deposit eggs and die. These can be killed during the winter by spraying with tar oil wash, thus weakening their life cycle. The control of water lily aphids in the pool, other than by washing off with clear water, is impossible.

SEASONAL MAINTENANCE

Spring
- Aquatic plants can be planted.
- Lift and divide water lilies and marginal plants as necessary.
- Take cuttings from submerged aquatics and replant where necessary.
- Sow the seeds of aquatic plants and bog garden subjects that are available from seed companies.
- Take stem cuttings of selected marginal aquatics. Increase water lilies from eyes.
- Repot and replace the compost of any plants that require attention, but do not need dividing.
- If the pond requires cleaning out, the spring is the best time to do so.

Summer
- Control filamentous algae by twisting out with a stick.
- Introduce or replace any plants as required.
- Remove faded blossoms from marginal plants.
- Remove surplus floating plants with a net.
- Fertilize the compost of established water lilies and marginals.
- Sow freshly collected seeds of aquatic plants.
- Cut back any excessive growth of aquatic plants.

Fall
- Collect and store plantlets and turions of appropriate aquatics ready for the winter.
- Net the pool to keep out leaves.
- Cut back faded marginal plants, but do not cut hollow-stemmed aquatics below water level or else they might rot.
- Take root cuttings of bog garden plants like primulas.

Winter
- Ensure that an area of the surface is kept free from ice to permit the escape of noxious gases that may harm fish.
- Spray trees of the plum and cherry family with a winter wash to kill off the overwintering generation of water lily aphids.

causing problems. Irrespective of whether there are trees in your garden, leaves will find their way in during the fall. They can blow in from neighboring gardens and always tend to swirl around and be pulled down as soon as they come into contact with water.

Some leaves are extremely toxic, not to plants, but to fish, and should be excluded by whatever means possible.

index

Note: Italic numbers indicate references to picture captions

algae 26, 33, *33*, 54, *61*, 62, *62*, 63
algicides 62, *62*
aphids, water lily 29, 63, *63*
astilbes 16, 54

baskets, planting 6, *31*, *38*, 42, *42*, 43, *44*, 45, 56, *56*
beaches 19, *42*, 43, *43*, 44, *60*
bentonite 6, 12, 46-47, *46*
birds 6, *12*, 18, 26, 43, 44, *45*
bog gardens 16-17, *17*, 40-41, *40*, *41*; *see also* plants, bog
brooks 24-25
burlap 56, 57

caddis flies 58
capacity, pool 29
cascades 26-27, 30
preformed units *31*
clay, puddle 6, 12, 30, 46
compost *45*, 56, 63
concrete 30, *35*, 60

dewponds 18, 46-47, *46*, *47*

edging 10, 49, 50-51, *50*, *51*; *see also* beaches

cobble 19, 23, *43*, *60*
grass *10*, 13, 50
paved 10, 11, 14, 34, *35*, 38, 50, *50*, *51*
planted 13, 30, 38, *39*
stone 11, *11*, 14, 38
electricity 28, 29, 32, *33*, *50*
erosion 61, *61*

ferns *17*, 26, 54
fertilizer 56
filters 32-33, *32*, 36-37, *36*, *37*, 52, *52*, 61
biological 33, 36, *36*, 37
ultraviolet 33, *33*, 36, *36*, 37, *53*
fish 11, 24, 42, 52, *52*, *53*, 56, *56*, 58-59, *58*, *59*, 63
stocking levels 59
fog effect *22*
fountains *33*, 36
frogs *19*, *43*

hostas 16, *21*, 41

islands 19, *42*, 44
floating 44-45, *44*, *45*
insects 6, *12*, 18, *19*, 24, 25, *42*, 43
irises *12*, *17*, *21*, 41, 54, 57

lakes 8-9, *9*
leaks 13, 46, 60
leaves, fallen *28*, 62-63, *62*
lighting 28

liners, pool 6, 13, 25, 26, 28, *28*, 29, 30, *30*, *31*, 38-39, *38*, *39*, 40, *41*, 42, *42*, *43*, 48, *48*, 49, *49*, 50, 60
measurements *30*
repairing 60, *60*

marigold, marsh *18*, 54

netting *62*, 63
nitrogen cycle 52, *52*

orchids *21*
oxygenation 32

paving *see* edging, paved
planting 56-57, *56*, *57*
plants 54-55, 56-57
bog *12*, 16, *19*, 25, 41, 54, 63
deep-water 29, 42, *42*, 55, 62
floating 55, 62, 63
marginal 6, *9*, *11*, *12*, 15, 16, *19*, *25*, 26, 29, *39*, 42, *42*, 54, 56, 61, 62, *62*, 63
submerged 42, *42*, 54, 62, 63
ponds
informal 10-11, *10*, *11*, 14, 50-51, *50*, *51*
natural 12-13, *12*, *13*, 14, *14*
semiformal 14-15, *15*
wildlife 18-19, 42-43, 58

pools
lined 38-39, *38*, *39*
preformed 6, 13, *28*, 30, *31*, 34-35, *34*, *35*, 38, 60
sunken 22-23, *23*
primulas *17*, *21*, 27, 41, 54, *55*, 63
pumps 22, 25, 28, 32-33, *32*, *33*, 36-37, 48, 49, *49*, 52, *53*, 61, *61*
maintenance 33
size 32

reeds 12, *12*, *42*
rocks 26, 30, *31*, 42, 48, 49

safety 28, 29
shelves, marginal *31*, *34*, 38, 42, 43
siting 28, *28*, 38
springs 22-23, *22*, *23*, 32
streams *22*, 24-25, *24*, 25
artificial 25, 30, 48-49, *48*, *49*

testing water 52, *53*
toads *19*, *43*

underlay 30, 38, *38*, *39*, 42, 48, 49

water lilies *9*, *11*, 12, 16, *42*, 55, *55*, *57*, *61*, 63
water meadows 20-21, *21*
waterfalls 26-27, *27*, 30, 32

Picture Credits
Eric Crichton: 4 (Mr and Mrs D. Wells, Dorset/NGS), 9 bottom (Mr and Mrs D. Edwards, Essex/NGS), 10 (Mrs U. Carr, Avon/NGS), 12 left (Simon and Kate Harman, RHS Hampton Court 1999), 15 bottom (Crockett & Summers, Dorset Water Lily Co, RHS Hampton Court 1999), 19 left, 20-21 (RHS Chelsea 1998), 21 bottom (Mr and Mrs Porteous, Dorset/NGS), 24 bottom (Longstock Gardens/NGS), 31, 34-35 (design: Carol Klein, RHS Chelsea 1999), 39 (Mr and Mrs J. Draper, Denbigh & Colwyn/NGS), 61 (Lady Johnson, Kent/NGS). **John Glover:** 8-9, 9 top, 11, 14, 19 right, 25, 26, 40, 57. **S. and O. Mathews:** 5, 6, 12 right, 16-17, 17 top, 17 bottom, 21 top, 24 top, 33, 47, 55 both, 59. **Clive Nichols Garden Pictures:** 1 (Paul Dyer, RHS Hampton Court 2001), 15 top (Greenhurst Garden, Sussex), 23 top (Christopher Costin, RHS Hampton Court 1995), 27 (Little Coopers, Hampshire), 53 (Carolyn Hubble). **Neil Sutherland:** 3, 7, 13, 18, 22, 23 bottom, 49.